Countries Around the World

Czech Republic

Charlotte Guillain

Heinemann Library
Chicago, Illinois

www.heinemannraintree.com
Visit our website to find out more information about Heinemann-Raintree books.

To order:

☎ Phone 888-454-2279

▣ Visit www.heinemannraintree.com to browse our catalog and order online.

Edited by Kate de Villiers and Vaarunika Dharmapala
Designed by Joanna Hinton-Malivoire
Original illustrations © Capstone Global Library Ltd 2011
Illustrated by Oxford Designers & Illustrators
Picture research by Ruth Blair
Originated by Capstone Global Library Ltd
Printed and bound in China by CTPS

15 14 13 12
10 9 8 7 6 5 4 3 2 1

Library of Congress Cataloging-in-Publication Data
Guillain, Charlotte.
  Czech Republic / Charlotte Guillain.
    p. cm.—(Countries around the world)
  Including bibliographical references and index.
  ISBN 978-1-4329-5200-6 (hardcover)—ISBN 978-1-4329-5225-9 (pbk.) 1. Czech Republic—Juvenile literature. I. Title.
  DB2011.G8 2012
  943.71—dc22   2010039271

Acknowledgments
We would like to thank the following for permission to reproduce photographs: Alamy p. **9** (© Lebrecht Music and Arts Photo Library), p. **10** (© akg-images), p. **12** (© Imagestate Media Partners Limited - Impact Photos), p. **21** (© Alex Hibbert), p. **23** (© Andrew Parker), p. **28** (© Peter Forsberg/CR), p. **39** (© Pictorial Press Ltd); Corbis p. **19** (© PETR JOSEK/Reuters), p. **29** (© Miroslav Zajíc); Shutterstock p. **5** (© Jozef Sedmak), pp. **7, 8** (© Kajano), p. **13** (© VOJTa Herout), p. **15** (© Jiri Papousek), p. **17** (© Daniel Prudek), p. **22** (© Peter Wollinga), p. **25** (© BESTWEB), p. **26** (© Tatonka), p. **27** (© Pavel Kosek), p. **31** (© Yvan), p. **32** (© Ales Nowak), p. **33** (© Elzbieta Sekowska), p. **35** (© Tyler Olson), p. **37** (© haak78), p. **46** (© Atlaspix).

Cover photograph of Prague Astronomical Clock reproduced with permission of Corbis (© Tetra Images).

We would like to thank Daniel Block for his invaluable help in the preparation of this book.

Every effort has been made to contact copyright holders of material reproduced in this book. Any omissions will be rectified in subsequent printings if notice is given to the publisher.

Disclaimer
All the Internet addresses (URLs) given in this book were valid at the time of going to press. However, due to the dynamic nature of the Internet, some addresses may have changed, or sites may have changed or ceased to exist since publication. While the author and publisher regret any inconvenience this may cause readers, no responsibility for any such changes can be accepted by either the author or the publisher.

Contents

Some words in the book are in bold, **like this**. You can find out what they mean by looking in the glossary.

Introducing the Czech Republic

What do you know about the Czech Republic? Is it the same as Czechoslovakia? You may have heard of its capital city, Prague, but do you know anything about the rest of the country? What do Czech people eat and how do they spend their free time? What does their country look like?

Small but spectacular

The Czech Republic is a small country in central Europe. It covers an area of 30,450 square miles (78,867 sq km), which is slightly smaller than the state of South Carolina. It is a country of beautiful cities with incredible architecture, a thriving café **culture**, and a vibrant arts scene. It has stunning countryside with large areas of forest, lakes, and rolling hills. The Czechs are proud of their artists, writers, and musicians, and the country produces some world-class sports stars.

New nation

The country has only existed since 1993, when Czechoslovakia split into the two nations of the Slovak Republic (Slovakia) and the Czech Republic. Czechoslovakia itself had only existed for 74 years before that. But the history of the Czech people and land stretches back over hundreds of years and involves stories of power and repression. Read on to find out what makes the Czech Republic and its people so remarkable and unique.

How to say...
Hello *Dobrý den!* (DOH-bree dehn)
Hi *Ahoj!* (ahoy)
How are you? *Jak se máte?* (yahk seh MAA-teh?)
Goodbye *Na shledanou!* (NAHSH-leh-dah-noh)
Yes *Ano* (AH-noh)
No *Ne* (neh)
Please/You're welcome *Prosím* (proseem)
Thank you *Děkuji* (dyekooyih)

The buildings in the capital city, Prague, are spectacular.

History: Repression and Rebirth

The history of the Czech people began with various **tribes** that came to central Europe from the east. By the 600s CE, the Slav tribe had become dominant. The Great Moravian **Empire** was set up in the 800s CE, covering Czech lands, Slovakia, and parts of Poland and Hungary. In 895 CE, the region of **Bohemia** separated from Great Moravia. This kingdom remained an independent or semi-independent state for the next 500 years, and the region of Bohemia is still the core of the Czech Republic.

Bohemia and the Golden Age

The Přemyslid **dynasty** began in about 850 CE with the first **Christian** ruler of Prague, Duke Bořivoj. The Přemyslid rulers brought order to the Czech lands. One of these rulers was Prince Václav, who is well known as King Wenceslas from the Christmas carol! But the Přemyslid rulers were threatened by the Holy Roman Empire. The Holy Roman Empire was a large territory in central Europe that had an **elected** emperor.

The Czech nation's "Golden Age" took place when Charles IV was king of Bohemia (1346–1378). He was also elected Holy Roman Emperor. During his reign he had many buildings, monuments, and educational and religious institutions built in Prague, and he promoted the Czech language.

KING CHARLES IV [1316-1378]

When Charles IV became King of Bohemia and Holy Roman Emperor in 1346, he was the most powerful ruler in Europe. He valued learning and founded Charles University in Prague in 1348. **Culture** flourished in Prague, and Charles worked hard to keep control and expand his empire.

Many places were named after Charles IV, including Charles Bridge, Karlstejn Castle, and the **spa** town of Karlovy Vary.

Changing beliefs

The **Roman Catholic** Church had a lot of power in Europe at this time. But during the 1300s, people questioned this power and began to change their religious beliefs. The preacher Jan Hus criticized the wealth and **corruption** of the church. His followers were called Hussites. Hus was eventually burned at the stake, leading to a rebellion and wars from 1419 to 1434.

This statue celebrates the preacher Jan Hus.

Habsburg takeover

In the 1300s, the Habsburgs were the most powerful family in Europe. In 1526, the Habsburg ruler Ferdinand I was elected king of Bohemia. The Habsburgs forced Czechs to return to Roman Catholic beliefs. The Thirty Years' War took place 1618–1648 and ended with the Catholics in power and the Czech lands in ruins. Czechs call the 200 years that followed "the Dark Ages."

The First Republic 1918–1938

The **Industrial Revolution** transformed the country in the 1800s. Industries grew—and so did a sense of Czech national identity. Under Habsburg rule, the dominant language and culture was German. But Czechs wanted more rights and, by the end of the 1800s, Tomaš Masaryk became an important political figure.

The first Czechoslovak Republic was set up after World War I in 1918, uniting Bohemia, Moravia, and Slovakia.

Tomaš Masaryk was Czechoslovakia's first president.

Daily life

Under Habsburg rule, only peasants used the Czech language. All academic and official work was done in German. But during the 1800s, the Czech language was revived. Ordinary people could enjoy and understand music, literature, and the theater. The National Theater opened in Prague in 1883, and the National Museum was founded in 1818.

Nazi occupation

By the 1930s, many people living near the German border wanted to become part of Germany. The German leader, Adolf Hitler, encouraged this, and in 1938 Britain and France agreed to let Germany take this land. They hoped this would avoid war. But in 1939 **Nazi** Germany invaded the rest of Czechoslovakia and Poland, and World War II began.

The German **SS** general Reinhard Heydrich was put in charge of Czechosolvakia. He treated Czechs very harshly and was **assassinated** by Czech resistance leaders in 1942. Hitler was so angry that he murdered the people of two whole Czech towns. Czech **Jews** were sent to the **ghetto** at Terezín and then taken to **concentration camps**, such as Auschwitz. Over 78,000 Czechoslovakian Jews died in the **Holocaust**.

German SS officer, Reinhard Heydrich (front right) was hated by the Czechs for his cruelty.

HELGA WEISSOVA [1929–]

Helga Weissova lived in the Jewish ghetto of Terezín as a child. The Nazis put Czech Jews there to work before sending them to camps to be killed. Helga drew and painted many pictures of life in the ghetto before she was sent to Auschwitz. She survived and is now a well-known Czech artist.

Key
- Communist countries after World War II
- Non-communist countries
- Country borders

0   300   600 kilometers
0   400 miles

ESTONIA
LATVIA
RUSSIA
LITHUANIA
RUSSIA
BELARUS
EAST GERMANY
POLAND
UKRAINE
CZECHOSLOVAKIA
MOLDAVIA
HUNGARY
ROMANIA
YUGOSLAVIA
BULGARIA
ALBANIA

N

This map shows which countries in Europe became communist after World War II.

Under communism

At the end of World War II the army of the **Soviet Union** helped to liberate the Czech lands. By 1946, the Czech **communists** were in power. At first they were popular with ordinary people. The **Cold War** had started, with the Soviet Union and its allies deeply suspicious of the **West**. The Soviet leader, Stalin, encouraged the Czech communists to take control of industries and farms. Many non-communists were imprisoned or executed, and an atmosphere of fear took over.

Prague Spring

People began to feel very unhappy with the government. The **economy** was also doing badly. The government tried to introduce **reforms** to improve the situation. But after the reforms failed, people began to protest against the government. In 1968, Alexander Dubĉek became leader and announced the end of **censorship**, and the right of people to criticize the government. This new time of freedom was known as the "Prague Spring."

The Soviet Union did not want Czechoslovakia to become a **democracy**, so they sent troops to stop the reforms. Many Czechs left the country before the borders were closed, and the communists took absolute control of people's lives again.

Velvet Revolution

Intellectuals and writers continued to protest against communism and many, including the **playwright** Václav Havel, were imprisoned for speaking out. In the late 1980s, a new Soviet leader, Mikhail Gorbachev, brought an atmosphere of change. The Velvet Revolution took place in November 1989, with a huge, peaceful demonstration across the country.

Thousands of people demonstrated in Wenceslas Square in Prague during the Velvet Revolution.

In 1989, Czechoslovakia became a democracy, with Václav Havel as president.

New nation

Czechoslovakia split into the Czech Republic and the Slovak Republic in 1993. Both countries joined the European Union (**EU**) in 2004. Since then, the economy of the Czech Republic has done well, despite the global **recession** that started in 2008. The strong economy has meant that most young Czech people have chosen to remain in their own country rather than looking for jobs elsewhere in the EU.

YOUNG PEOPLE

Under communism most young people didn't hear or see much Western music or fashion. But many Czech rock musicians performed their own songs that rebelled against authority. After the Prague Spring of 1968, many music clubs were closed, and bands were forced to change the music they played.

Regions and Resources: Lakes, Forests, and Caves

The Czech Republic is a **landlocked** country. The western region of **Bohemia** is made up of rolling plains, hills, and plateaus that are surrounded by low mountains. In the east, the Moravian-Silesian region is very hilly. The capital city of the Czech Republic is Prague, in central Bohemia.

A number of other countries surround the Czech Republic. Germany borders the west of the country, with Poland to the northeast, Austria to the south, and Slovakia to the southeast. This area of central Europe has a climate made up of warm summers and cold winters.

This map shows the land height above sea level of the Czech Republic and its neighbors.

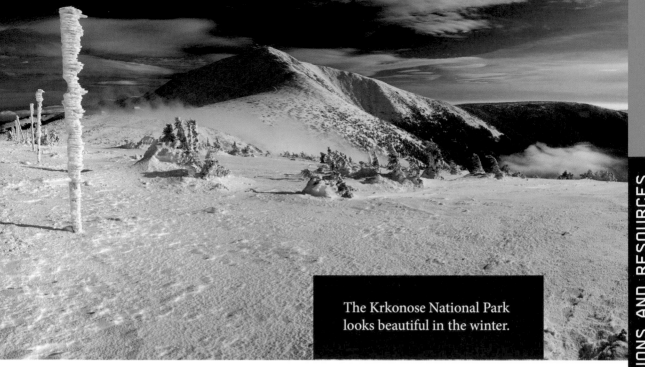

The Krkonose National Park looks beautiful in the winter.

Landscape and features

The Czech people are very proud of their forests, which cover 34.3 percent of the country. The largest lake in the Czech Republic is Černé Jezero, which means "Black Lake." It has a surface area of 220,060 square yards (184,000 square meters). Sněžka is the highest mountain, at 5,256 feet (1,602 meters). It is part of the Krkonose mountain range found along the border with Poland. The longest river in the country is the Vltava, which is 267 miles (430 kilometers) long. This river flows through the center of Prague. Other rivers include the Odra, Morava, and Labe.

How to say...

cave *jeskyně* (YES-kee-nyeh)
forest *les* (less)
hill *hora* (hoara)
lake *jezero* (YEZ-eh-roh)
meadow *louka* (looka)
mountain *horský* (HOR-skee)
river *řeka* (rzh-EH-ka)

Regions of the Czech Republic

The Czech Republic has 13 regions within the 2 distinct areas of Bohemia and Moravia-Silesia:

Bohemia

The region of Bohemia has an area of 20,367 square miles (52,750 square kilometers) and a population of around 6.25 million. As well as the capital city of Prague, there are many interesting towns and cities in Bohemia. Plzeň, in the west, is the largest city in Bohemia besides Prague and is famous for its beer production. Český Krumlov, in the south, is a town with beautiful architecture and is recognized as a **World Heritage site**. Karlovy Vary is a well-known **spa** city in the west with many hot springs and treatment centers.

In the Bohemian countryside, the Šumava mountains in the southwest are covered in pine forest and are popular with hikers. In the north of the region, České Švýcarsko is a hilly, forested area with incredible sandstone rock formations. In the east of Bohemia is the beautiful area of Česky Raj, with its forests, lakes, sandstone rocks, and the Krkonoše mountains.

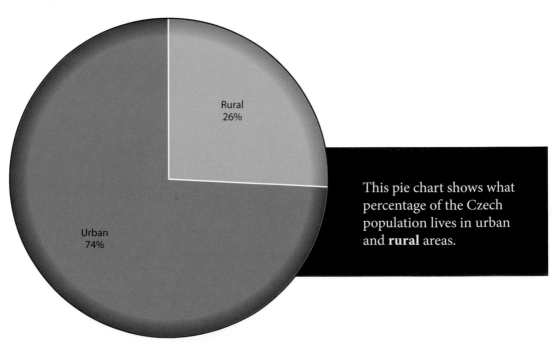

Rural
26%

Urban
74%

This pie chart shows what percentage of the Czech population lives in urban and **rural** areas.

Česky Raj is famous for
its stunning landscape.

Moravian-Silesian region

The second and third biggest cities in the Czech Republic, Brno and Ostrava, are found in the Moravian-Silesian region. Brno is the regional capital and is an industrial city with many factories. Ostrava used to be a center for coal mining and steel production, but is now a popular tourist destination.

Outside the cities, the countryside is hilly and forested. Moravsky Kras is an area of limestone caves near Brno where many people like to explore. Beskydy is an area of wooded countryside close to Ostrava. The Jeseníky mountains continue the Bohemian Krknose range in the north.

The economy

The Czech Republic has enjoyed a stable **economy** since it became a member of the **EU**. The country has a good location in the center of Europe and **exports** goods such as machinery, vehicles, raw materials, and chemicals. The Czech government has managed the economy well through the global economic crisis of 2008. Tourism has become an important source of income for many Czechs, especially in Prague.

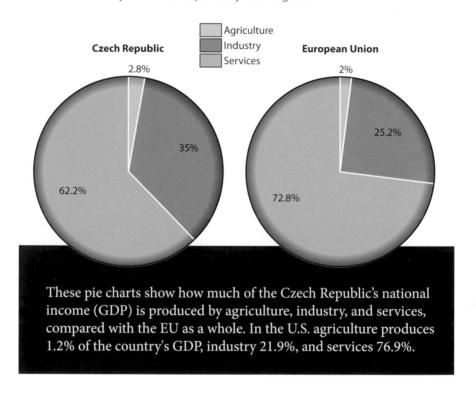

These pie charts show how much of the Czech Republic's national income (GDP) is produced by agriculture, industry, and services, compared with the EU as a whole. In the U.S. agriculture produces 1.2% of the country's GDP, industry 21.9%, and services 76.9%.

Industry and natural resources

Key industries in the Czech Republic are the production of motor vehicles, metals, machinery and equipment, glass, and **armaments**. In the past, coal mining and power production using coal were important to the economy, but environmental concerns have forced a reduction in these industries. However, hard coal and brown coal (lignite) are still mined in some areas.

Important natural resources include kaolin (clay), graphite, and timber. Nearly 39 percent of the country's land is used to grow crops.

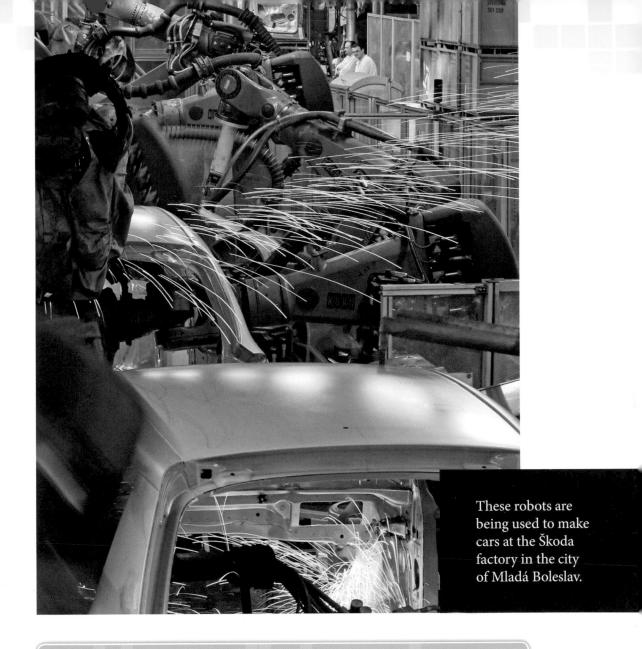

These robots are being used to make cars at the Škoda factory in the city of Mladá Boleslav.

EMIL VON ŠKODA (1839–1900)

Emil von Škoda was an engineer. In 1869, he bought and developed a factory in Plzeň that made machine guns. Many of the arms made at his Škoda Works were used in the two world wars. After 1945, the government took over the factory and the car-making section went on to make Škoda cars. Many in the **West** thought Škodas were an underpowered joke, but they still sold well in many countries. The company was bought by Volkswagen in 1991.

Wildlife: Land of the Lynx

There are many national parks in the Czech Republic, where wildlife is protected. These include the Bílé Karpaty, or White Carpathians, full of wild meadows that are home to rare species of plants and insects. České Švýcarsko is a park with sandstone formations, and Jizerské Hory in the north is a mountainous area where many trees and plants are protected.

The Šumava National Park

The Šumava National Park in the south of **Bohemia** is an important **habitat** for many animals and plants. The park and the preserved land around it have an area of 645 square miles (1,670 square kilometers).

In the streams and rivers of Šumava, there are rare animals such as otters, lampreys, and crayfish. Birds in the park include kingfishers, white-backed woodpeckers, the lesser-spotted eagle, and the peregrine falcon. There are many mammals in Šumava National Park, both large and small. Small mammals include rare species of bat, the northern birch mouse, pine marten, badger, and wild boar. Bigger animals, such as the red deer and roe deer, are joined by moose at certain times of year.

How to say...

badger *jezevec* (yez-e-vech)
bat *odpálkovat* (od-pahl-ko-vat)
bird *pták* (p-tahk)
deer *jelen* (YEL-en)
fish *ryba* (REE-ba)
lynx *rys* (rees)
mouse *myš* (meesh)
squirrel *veverka* (ve-VAIR-ka)

The northern lynx, Europe's largest feline **predator**, can be found at Šumava. The lynx population was destroyed by humans in the late 1800s, but it was reintroduced to the park in the 1980s.

Threatened species

There are a number of **endangered** species in the Czech Republic, including the Danube crested newt, the Eurasian curlew, the Alpine shrew, and a number of bats. Many plants and insects are also endangered because their habitat has been destroyed by human activity. In 2010, the Czech Republic used the International Year of Biodiversity to highlight the threat to these species. The Czech Environment Ministry launched a campaign to make people more aware of their natural environment.

The Eurasian curlew is an endangered species that needs protection.

The environment

Industry, mining, and agriculture have all caused pollution in the Czech Republic. During **communist** rule the air was heavily polluted by sulphur dioxide from burning lignite (brown coal) that was used as an energy source. In the late 1980s, a program was introduced to cut this down. The country has also tried to reduce its carbon dioxide **emissions**.

In the past, acid rain and air pollution destroyed forests in the north of the country. Mining and agriculture have also **eroded** the land. Today, the need to protect the environment has to be balanced against the country's economic growth. When the Czech Republic joined the **EU** it had to follow regional rules that help reduce pollution.

These trees have been damaged by acid rain.

YOUNG PEOPLE

The Czech Environmental Partnership Foundation works to support **sustainable development** projects. It works in schools helping teachers and young people to improve their environment and save resources. Some schools have built nature trails or created outdoor classrooms. Others have looked at transportation and road safety. In 2009, there was a campaign for schools to provide more organic food for students.

Infrastructure: From Money to Mud Baths

Since the Velvet Revolution in 1989, the Czech government has been a parliamentary **democracy**. People **elect** a president who acts as **head of state** for a five-year term. A prime minister is elected to lead the government. Parliament is responsible for making the final decisions on new government proposals.

There are 200 members of the lower house of parliament, called the House of Representatives, who are elected for a four-year term. The 81 members of the upper house, called the Senate, are elected for six-year terms. Two deputy prime ministers coordinate work between the various government departments.

The Czech Republic is a member of **NATO**, the World Trade Organization, and the International Monetary Fund.

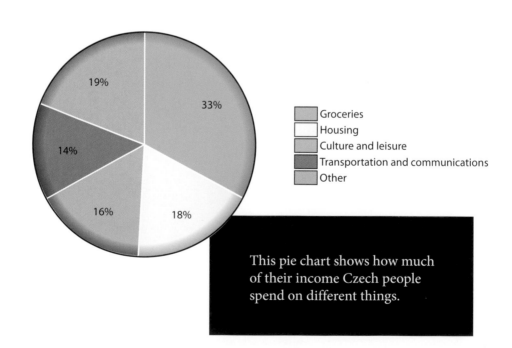

Groceries
Housing
Culture and leisure
Transportation and communications
Other

This pie chart shows how much of their income Czech people spend on different things.

Money

The **currency** in the Czech Republic is the crown (*koruna* or Kč). There are 1, 2, 5, 10, 20, and 50 Kč coins and 50, 100, 200, 500, 1,000, 2,000, and 5,000 Kč banknotes. Coins called hellers (*haléř*) are no longer used. The Czech Republic plans to move from the crown and use the **euro** in the future.

The pictures on Czech crowns show many famous people from the country's history.

EMA DESTINNOVÁ (1878–1930)

On the 2,000 Kč note there is a picture of Ema Destinnová. She was an opera singer who became one of the world's most famous **sopranos**. She traveled widely, but when she returned to her hometown of Stráž during World War I, she was kept under house arrest for having revolutionary ideas. After the war, she toured Europe again and helped to make Czech opera and music popular.

School

Czech children have to start elementary school at the age of six, but many go to preschool before this. They stay at elementary school for nine years, split into two stages. At the end of elementary school they receive a certificate called a *vysvědčení*. Students can then choose from three different types of high school, and then go on to **vocational** training or a university.

Czech schoolchildren don't have to wear uniforms. They don't wear their outdoor shoes in school, but wear special slippers indoors. Many schools start very early in the morning, with some classes beginning at 7:15 a.m. Most lessons happen in the morning, and then there is a cooked lunch. After lunch most children play sports or do other outdoor activities. Children have a long summer vacation and two shorter vacations at Christmas and Easter.

These students are attending a Czech high school.

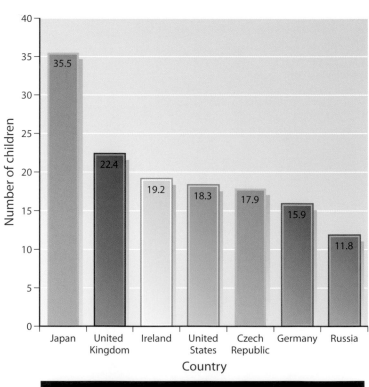

The bar chart above shows the average class size for 13-year-olds in various countries, including the Czech Republic.

Health

Under the **communist** government, the Czech health care system became quite outdated. Since 1989, many new hospitals have been built and the system has been modernized. Today, Czech people can choose public or private health insurance. They are then able to choose which doctors and hospitals treat them. Life expectancy has also increased. The World Health Organization placed the Czech Republic 48th out of 190 countries in its ranking of world health systems in 2000.

Daily life

Many people in the Czech Republic visit natural **spa**s to improve their health. There are more than 35 spas in the country and doctors often prescribe treatments for their patients. People drink water that is rich in minerals and bathe in warm mineral springs. Other treatments involve wrapping patients in mud or peat! This woman (right) is collecting spring water to drink in Karlovy Vary, a famous spa town to the west of Prague.

Culture: "Every Czech Is a Musician"

Music is very important to the Czech people. There is an expression, "*Co Čech, to muzikant,*" which means "Every Czech is a musician." The **classical** composer Mozart had many of his operas performed in Prague for the first time. Famous Czech composers include Leoš Janáček, Antonín Dvořák, and Bedřich Smetana, and there is a festival of classical music in Prague every May. Folk and traditional music also plays a big part in Czech people's lives, as does modern rock and pop music.

YOUNG PEOPLE

Several music festivals take place in the Czech Republic over the summer. Trutnov was one of the first open air festivals in the country, and features Czech and foreign bands. Sonisphere is for heavy metal fans, with many famous international bands playing. Colors of Ostrava is a festival that welcomes a range of music from all over the world.

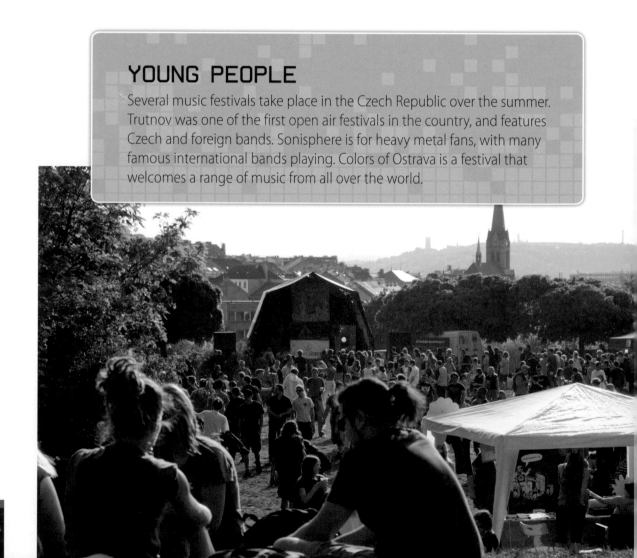

Art

One of the most famous Czech artists was the painter and poster artist Alfons Mucha (1860–1939). He worked in a style known as **Art Nouveau**, often producing beautiful advertisements for products, such as cookies and chocolate. Josef Sudek (1896–1976) was a well-known Czech photographer who took beautiful photographs of Prague.

Drama

Czech people often go to see plays and movies. The ex-President Václav Havel is a **playwright** who was often jailed by the **communists** for the ideas explored in his drama. There is a strong theatrical tradition that includes ballet and puppet theater. The Czech movie industry is flourishing, and Czech directors such as Miloš Forman are famous around the world.

This is the photographer Josef Sudek in 1971.

Books

The Czech writer Karel Čapek wrote an early type of **science fiction** and invented the word "robot." He died on Christmas day in 1938. Čapek was married to the writer and actress Olga Scheinpflugová, who wrote novels, children's books, poetry, and plays.

Franz Kafka was a Jewish writer whose world famous novels include *The Metamorphosis*, *The Trial*, and *The Castle*. His books describe very strange and frustrating events. Milan Kundera has written about life in communist times, as has the children's writer Peter Sís. Petr Horáček produces beautifully illustrated children's picture books, often featuring animals.

Sports

Many Czech people enjoy playing and watching ice hockey, soccer, tennis, and volleyball. Some of the most famous Czech sportspeople have played tennis. Tomas Berdych and Petra Kvitová both regularly reach the final stages of grand slam tournaments, such as Wimbledon. They are following in the footsteps of tennis legends such as Martina Navrátilová and Ivan Lendl.

Other famous Czech sports stars include Jaromír Jágr, who played ice hockey in the United States for many years, Petr Čech, who plays soccer at the highest level, and the Olympic-gold-winning decathlete Roman Šebrle.

Leisure

It is traditional for many Czech people who live in cities to have a cottage (*chata*) in the countryside. They go there for weekends and vacations to relax, pick mushrooms, and grow fruit and vegetables. Other **rural** activities include hiking and camping.

In the cities, many people go to cafés, movies, concerts, and the theater, which isn't too expensive. Around 65.5 percent of the population is connected to the Internet, and many people enjoy playing computer games.

Petra Kvitová plays tennis in the top tournaments, including the French Open.

Traditions

On December 5, adults dress up as St. Nicholas, the Devil, and angels and visit children at home. Children who have been bad are supposed to get a lump of coal, but really everyone gets a present! Czechs celebrate Christmas on Christmas eve, eating a dinner of a fish called carp. They buy the carp live and keep it in the bath until they are ready to cook it.

Food

Traditional Czech food tends to be very meaty and filling. A classic Czech meal is pork, cabbage, and dumplings. Vegetarians can try fried cheese (*smaženy syr*) or potato pancakes (*bramborák*). There are also some delicious sweet Czech foods, such as fruit dumplings, *buchty* (small buns filled with jam), and apple strudel. Czech beer is also world famous.

How to say...

Enjoy your meal *Dobrou chut* (DO-brooh khutye)
apple *jablko* (YAB-l-koh)
bread *chléb* (KHLEH-b)
meat *maso* (MA-so)
milk *mléko* (MLAY-koh)
potato *brambora* (bram-bor-a)
cabbage *zelí* (ZE-lee)
cheese *sýr* (seer)
dumplings *knedlíky* (k-ned-LEE-kee)

At Easter, people decorate eggs and wear red to symbolize happiness and new life. One Easter tradition involves twisting painted willow twigs together. Boys then chase girls and beat their legs with the twigs!

On April 30, many rural Czechs make bonfires on hilltops. This marks the beginning of spring. However, it comes from a much nastier custom. In medieval times, women were burned if people thought they were witches.

Potato pancakes (Bramborák)

Ask an adult to help you make this.

Ingredients:

- 2 pounds potatoes
- 2 eggs
- 4 cloves garlic
- handful of parsley
- 1 large onion
- 1 tablespoon of milk
- 1 cup flour
- 2–3 teaspoons oil
- a pinch of salt and pepper

What to do:

1. Peel and chop the potatoes and soak them in water for 15 minutes.
2. Chop the onion, garlic, and parsley and put them in a bowl.
3. Shred the potatoes using a grater or food processor.
4. Pick up the shredded potatoes in your hands and squeeze out the liquid before putting them into the bowl with the onion, garlic, and parsley.
5. Pour the milk over the top of the mixture.
6. Stir in the eggs and then the flour to make a sticky batter.
7. Heat the oil in a nonstick pan and put a spoonful of batter into the pan to make a pancake. Fry for five minutes over a low to medium heat and then turn it over. Repeat until all the batter is used. Serve as a side dish.

The Czech Republic Today

Life has been good for many Czechs since the end of **communism**. The country has developed and most people enjoy a good life. Around nine percent of Czechs are living in poverty—the lowest rate in the **EU**. However, some groups, such as the **Roma** people, have suffered as things have changed. They are often treated badly and have trouble finding work.

Czechs can seem quite serious-minded people. They value education, and can be very private. But they also have a quirky sense of humor and love relaxing with their families and friends. They are very proud of their **culture**, and love their countryside, cities, and cuisine.

On the whole, the outlook is positive for the Czech Republic. In the future, the country hopes to adopt the **euro** as its **currency**, joining many other European countries, such as France, Germany, and Ireland. The Czech people are proud of the achievements of their small nation, and many still remember the hardships experienced during World War II and communist rule. Why not find out more about this fascinating country and its people?

How to say...

The Czech language can seem hard to pronounce! There are several letters in the Czech alphabet with accents that we don't have in the English language. Here is a guide on how to pronounce some of them:

á - an "ah" sound as in "father"

ě - a "ye" sound, as in "yes"

š - a "sh" sound, as in "ship"

č - a "ch" sound as in "chocolate"

ž - sounds like the "sh" sound in the word "treasure"

ř - like a mixture of "r" and " ž."

Trams are a great way to get around Prague quickly.

Fact File

Official name:	Czech Republic
Official language:	Czech
Capital city:	Prague (Praha)
Bordering countries:	Germany, Austria, the Slovak Republic (Slovakia), Poland
Population:	10,201,707
Largest cities (populations):	Prague (1,249,026) Brno (371,399) Ostrava (335,425) Plzeň (169,935)
Urban population:	73% of total population
Birth rate:	8.76 births per 1,000 people
Life expectancy (total):	77.01 years
Life expectancy (men):	73.74 years
Life expectancy (women):	80.48 years
Ethnic groups (percentage):	Czech (90.4%) Moravian (3.7%) Slovak (1.9%) other (4%)
Religion (percentage):	**Roman Catholic** (26.8%) Protestant 2.1% no religion (59%) unspecified (8.8%) other (3.3%)
Internet users:	6,680,800 (65.5 % of population)
Military service:	voluntary for everyone aged 18–28
Type of government:	parlimentary **democracy**
National animal:	double-tailed lion
National tree:	linden

Climate:	warm summers and cold winters
Area (total):	30,450 square miles (78,867 square kilometers)
land:	29,825 square miles (77,247 square kilometers)
water:	625 square miles (1,620 square kilometers)
Mountains:	Sněžka—5,256 feet (1,602 meters)
	Luční hora—5,102 feet (1,555 meters)
	Praděd—4,892 feet (1,491 meters)
Major rivers:	Vltava—267 miles (430 kilometers)
	Odra (within the Czech Republic)—69 miles (112 kilometers)
Highest elevation:	Snezka—5,256 feet (1,602 meters)
Lowest elevation:	Elbe River—377 feet (115 meters)
Currency:	Czech crown (koruna)
Resources:	coal, kaolin, clay, graphite, timber
Major industries:	vehicles, metals, machinery, glass, **armaments**
Imports:	machinery, raw materials, chemicals
Exports:	machinery, raw materials, chemicals
Units of measurement:	metric

The Cathedral of St. Peter and Paul (center) stands in the old part of the city of Brno.

Famous Czechs

Franz Kafka (writer)
Martina Navrátilová (tennis player)
Ivan Lendl (tennis player)
Václav Havel (ex-president and **playwright**)
Eva Herzigová (model)
Tomas Berdych (tennis player)
Petra Kvitová (tennis player)

Miloš Forman (film director)
Milan Kundera (writer),
Peter Sís (writer)
Petr Horáček (writer and illustrator)
Helga Weissova (artist)
Helena Houdová (model)
Petr Čech (soccer player)

National holidays

January 1	New Year's Day
March/April	Easter
May 1	May Day
May 8	Liberation Day
July 5	Day of the Apostles St. Cyril and St. Methodius
July 6	Anniversary of the Martyrdom of Jan Hus
September 28	Czech Statehood Day
October 28	Independence Day
November 17	Freedom and Democracy Day
December 24–26	Christmas

The Czech Republic national anthem

The national anthem of the Czech Republic is called *Where Is My Home?* It was first adopted in 1918, when the country was known as Czechoslovakia. Then in 1993, it became the anthem of the Czech Republic.

> *Where is my home, where is my home?*
> *Water roars across the meadows,*
> *Pinewoods rustle among crags,*
> *The garden is glorious with spring blossom,*
> *Paradise on earth it is to see.*
> *And this is that beautiful land,*
> *The Czech land, my home,*
> *The Czech land, my home.*

The Famous Czech writer Franz Kafka grew up in Prague.

Timeline

BCE is short for before the Common Era. BCE is added after a date and means that the date occurred before the birth of Jesus Christ, for example, 450 BCE.

CE is short for Common Era. CE is added after a date and means that the date occurred after the birth of Jesus Christ, for example, 720 CE.

846	Start of the Great Moravian **Empire**
895	Magyar invasion, the end of Great Moravian Empire
929	St. Wenceslas is killed by his brother, Boleslav the Cruel
950	Holy Roman Emperor Otto I forces **Bohemia** to become part of his empire
1306	End of the Přemyslid **dynasty**
1346	Charles IV becomes king of Bohemia and Holy Roman Emperor
1378	Vaclav IV becomes ruler
1402	Jan Hus starts preaching in Prague
1415	Jan Hus is burned at the stake
1526	King Louis is defeated and killed by the Turks, leaving no heir. Ferdinand I becomes king of Bohemia.
1618	Two nobles are thrown out of a window in Prague Castle. This triggers the start of the Thirty Years' War.
1648	The end of the Thirty Years' War
1651	More than 200 people are burned as witches
1787	Mozart's opera *Don Giovanni* is performed for the first time in Prague
1915	Franz Kafka publishes his story *Metamorphosis*, about a man who wakes up and finds he has turned into an insect
1918	End of World War I. First Czechoslovak Republic (Czechoslovakia) is declared. Tomáš Masaryk becomes president.

1919	International peacemakers declare the Sudetenland is part of Czechoslovakia
1929	The Wall Street Crash in the United States. The Czech **economy** is in chaos.
1937	Tomas Masaryk dies
1938	Germany occupies the Sudetenland
1939	Germany invades the rest of Czechoslovakia. The start of World War II.
1942	Reinhard Heydrich is assassinated by Czech rebels
1945	Czechoslovakia is liberated by the Russians
1948	**Communist** government is firmly established in Czechoslovakia
1968	The Prague Spring. **Reforms** are crushed when Russian tanks invade.
1978	Martina Navrátilová wins the first of nine tennis singles titles at Wimbledon
1989	The fall of the Berlin Wall and the Velvet Revolution in Czechoslovakia
1993	Czechoslovakia split into the Czech Republic and Slovakia. The Czech Republic is an independent state.
2004	The Czech Republic joins the **EU**
2009	The Czech Republic takes over EU presidency for a six-month term

Glossary

armament weapon used in war

Art Nouveau style of art popular in the late 1800s, often using stylized natural forms

assassinate murder, often for political reasons

Bohemia historical and former kingdom in the Czech Republic

censorship examination and control of information

classical serious, artistic music, often played by an orchestra or piano

Christian related to the religion based on the teachings of Christ, or a person of that religion

Cold War tension and conflict between communist and non-communist countries after World War I

communism social system where all people in a country share work and property. People who practice communism are called communists.

concentration camp prison and death camps where people were sent during World War II

corruption dishonest, self-serving activity

culture practices, traditions, and beliefs of a society

currency banknotes and coins accepted in exchange for goods and services

democracy system of government where the people of a country elect representatives to a parliament

dynasty series of emperors, kings, or queens belonging to the same family

economy to do with the money, industry, and jobs in a country

elect choose by voting

emission amount of pollution caused by the burning of fuels

empire group of countries ruled by a single government or ruler

endangered in danger of extinction

erode wear away

euro type of currency used in many European countries

EU (European Union) organization of European countries with shared political and economic aims

export transport and sell goods to another country

ghetto area in a city where a minority group lives separately

habitat environment where a plant or animal lives

head of state main public representative of a country, such as a queen or a president

Holocaust mass murder of millions of Jews and other minority groups during World War II

Industrial Revolution period during the 1700s and 1800s when major technological changes happened rapidly in Europe

intellectual academic and intelligent person

Jew person of the Jewish religion, ethnicity, or culture. Jewish people trace their roots back to the ancient Hebrew people of Israel.

landlocked country with no coastline

NATO (North Atlantic Treaty Organization) organization that includes the United States, Canada, and many European countries in which members give each other military help

Nazi member of the National Socialist Party in Germany in the 1930s and 1940s

playwright writer of play scripts

predator animal that hunts and feeds on other animals

recession decline in business and industry

reform improve by making changes

Roma minority group in Europe, also known as gypsies

Roman Catholic type of Christianity with the Pope as leader

rural in the countryside

science fiction type of literature that imagines how science could affect the world and other planets

soprano highest singing voice

Soviet Union communist state made up of Russia and its former empire, in existence between 1922 and 1991

spa health resort, often built around a mineral spring

SS (Schutzstaffel), a brutal Nazi military organization

sustainable development use of resources that does not damage the environment and will also be available in the future

tribe independent social group, historically often made up of nomadic peoples

World Heritage site place of cultural importance that is protected by a United Nations agency

vocational related to a profession or occupation

West refers to a group of developed nations with similar political systems and values, including the United States, the European Union, Canada, Australia, and New Zealand

Find Out More

Books

Bultje, Jan Willem. *Looking at the Czech Republic*. Minneapolis, MN: Oliver Press, 2006.

Docalavich, Heather. *Czech Republic*. Broomall, PA: Mason Crest Publishers, 2005.

Pundyk, Grace. *Welcome to the Czech Republic*. New York: Gareth Stevens, 2005.

Sioras, Efstathia, and Michael Spilling. *Czech Republic, 2nd edition*. Tarrytown, NY: Marshall Cavendish, 2009.

Sis, Peter. *The Wall: Growing Up Behind the Iron Curtain*. New York: Farrar, Straus and Giroux, 2007.

Van Cleaf, Kristin. *Czech Republic*. Edina, MN: Checkerboard Books, 2007.

Websites

http://www.state.gov/r/pa/ei/bgn/3237.htm

This website of the United States Department of State has plenty of information about the Czech Republic.

http://news.bbc.co.uk/2/hi/europe/country_profiles/1108489.stm

This BBC website includes a profile page on the country of the Czech Republic, including information on its leaders and media.

www.czech.cz

The Czech Republic's official website has plenty of information about life in the Czech Republic, as well as some great places to visit.

http://www.cia.gov/library/publications/the-world-factbook/geos/ez.html

The website of the CIA World Factbook is full of useful information about the Czech Republic.

Places to visit

If you ever get the chance to go to the Czech Republic, here are just some of the many places you could visit:

Petřín Hill, Prague

Travel to the top of the hill by cable car for fantastic views of the city, then walk down and enjoy the park.

Prague Castle

This huge castle is full of history and amazing buildings. You can watch the changing of the guards and relax in the gardens. You can also visit the Museum of the Miniature here, where you have to view all the exhibits through a magnifying glass!

Old Town Square, Prague

Visit the Old Town Hall in this historic square in Prague on the hour to watch the moving figures come out of the astronomical clock.

Museum of Marionettes, Prague

This museum is full of puppets and tells you about the history of this type of theater.

Karlstejn Castle

This castle near Prague was built by Charles IV.

Cesky Raj

Enjoy trekking and exploring the lakes, forests, and meadows in this region. The town of Jicin is worth a visit and is known as the "town of fairy tales."

Topic Tools

You can use these topic tools for your school projects. Trace the map onto a sheet of paper, using the thick black outlines to guide you.

A blue triangle was added to the Czech flag to make it different from the flag of Poland. Copy the flag design and then color in your picture. Make sure you use the right colors!

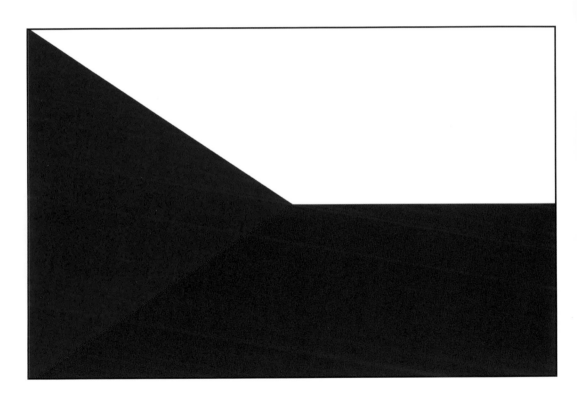

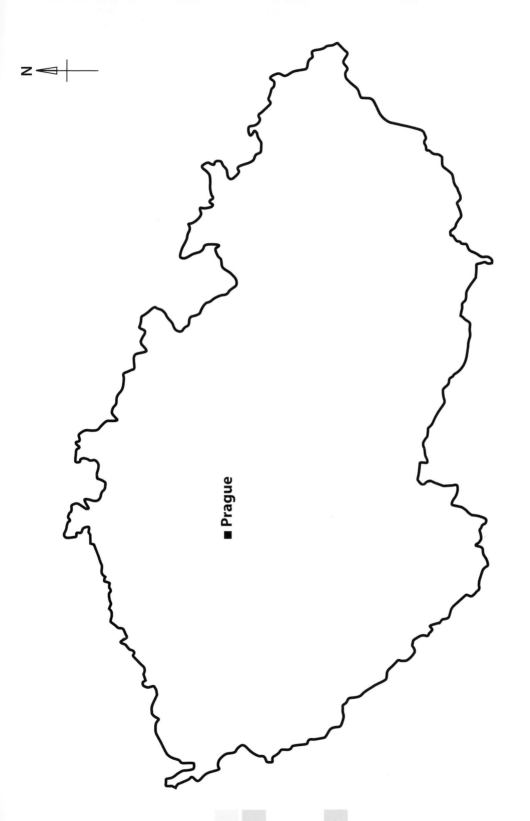

■ Prague

N

Index

Titles in the series